POETRY *FROM* DOWN SOUTH

John Wilson Powe Huggins

Poetry from Down South
Copyright © 2020 by John Wilson Powe Huggins

ISBN-13: Paperback: 978-1-64749-251-9

All rights reserved. No part of this publication may be reproduced, distributed, or transmitted in any form or by any means, including photocopying, recording, or other electronic or mechanical methods, without the prior written permission of the publisher or author, except in the case of brief quotations embodied in critical reviews and certain other noncommercial uses permitted by copyright law.

Although every precaution has been taken to verify the accuracy of the information contained herein, the author and publisher assume no responsibility for any errors or omissions.No liability is assumed for damages that may result from the use of information contained within.

Printed in the United States of America

GoTo Publish

GoToPublish LLC
1-888-337-1724
www.gotopublish.com
info@gotopublish.com

In loving memory of my niece, Anna Owens Linton.

Always Be Nice

I woke up to this morning and wondered how today would turn out.
I wondered if I would be the hero or the mad man who cries and shouts.
I wanted to know, so I got out of my bed to find out.

As I started out the door, my mother gave me her daily advice.
Be kind to everyone and always be nice.
So I started out to tackle the day, with this in mind.
The day was finally over, and I found out what I wanted to find.

I turned out to be a hero.
It doesn't take brains or looks, we all know.
Just take my advice,
Be kind to everyone and always be nice.

Anna, Darling

I heard the news early this morning.
I heard my niece, Anna, had passed away.
We will remember her and cry for her from this day.

I always thought she was a prize that was given to me for life.
She was a friend to everyone with her kindness.
She did not have to think twice.
She loved her pearls.
She was a southern girl.
She always had her special smile for you.
Most importantly, she was a Christian too.

It seems that the people that die
Are the ones you love the most.
Maybe not, maybe so.
But in Heaven,
Jesus will know them and be their host.

Anna was so young and favored her mother.
There was no one else like her,
None, no other!

She is in Heaven, she wouldn't boast.
Frank, her deceased uncle, should be her host.
She might even meet John Lennon.
Her act toward him would not be pretending.
Imagine, if he did not believe in Heaven or hell?
But I know Anna, she could tell !!

We will see her again soon, when the Rapture comes.
Jesus will call us up to Heaven, most everyone.
Anna did not wait long in her grave.
She was a good girl.
She did not much misbehave!

Praise The Flag of the United States

The only thing left is a flag that flies.
There's no more country,
Nobody left alive.
The only thing left is a flag,
And the country that died.

We sing our Star Spangled Banner,
With victory for us all.
We know the flag is not going to fall.

Well it never fails, just as well.
The flag still flies,
While our country has died.

Someone must have dropped the bomb.
The nuclear bomb.
Where am I coming from?
This act should never come true,
Because I love my country and flag, don't you?
No more nuclear war, too!
Hail to The Flag of the United States!

Just Say NO to Hand Guns, Too

Don't come near me, waving that thing around.
What are you doing, with that gun in your hand?
It could put someone under the ground !!

You might like to drink your liquor and booze,
But if you have a gun, you might lose.
You could end up killing yourself, or someone else.
I would NOT even purchase one myself.

Word to the wise.
 It could save lives.
It might be your own.
If you leave them alone.

What is a Dream Catcher ?

It looks like a black light poster to me.
That is from the sixties and seventies.
You can believe nothing of what you hear,
And half of what you see.
But it looks like a black light poster to me.

You see it sifts out your dreams,
In and around the ring.
Your thoughts and dreams come back to you.
Into your head.
All the better, while in the bed.

This dream catcher captured horror faces and monsters.
In the ring, in a dream.
They are shifted away.
 Out of the ring.
 Out of your head.
They become good dreams.
Washing away these horrors and bad things.

It could be used as an idol.
But that part is in the Bible.
The turquoise is for good luck.
It is just hanging there, that is enough.
At the bottom of the dream catcher, there is a feather.
Where the good luck dreams are filtered
Back to the person forever!

Time Has Run Out

Way up into the future, time has run out.
We don't know it yet.
We haven't traveled that far in time yet.
Don't stand there crying.
It makes sense if we keep on trying.
Is it going to be the Rapture that will take place?
Or is it going to be science and outer space?
Because the Rapture may come soon,
In Heaven, there will be plenty of room.

Time hasn't run out yet.
Maybe in the Rapture, you don't believe.
Something else could take place
In the time here-after, please.

I don't know, but let us begin.
Way up in the future, time will end.
There are chances that a nuclear holocaust could begin,
If we travel that far up in time, and back again.
Yes, we could stop some of the world's destructive acts.
We would need all countries to compromise the facts.

Summer Ends

Summer is giving its last day's "good-bye".
Fall doesn't even feel like giving it a try.
You can still hear the summer's nature cry.
You can hear the birds sing as summer days go by.
You may still smell the honey suckle left in the air.
I guess it is trying to die.

The cotton fields were not picked all the way.
You may still smell the poison for bugs in the air.
When you travel to the beach or on vacation, you will see
All the crops from the car window, easily.

Because tobacco may kill you dead,
My Grandpa grew cotton instead.
It is harvest time when these signs are read.
Fall is in the air.
The tobacco and cotton fields are getting bare.

Coming Home

You can go home again.
But you really can't go back.
The whole scene was kind of mean.
I left my home when I was sixteen.

I kissed my Mom goodbye in my dorm room.
I didn't even get time to cry.
As she left, I thought to run after her.
But my mind started running faster than her.

After she was gone, I didn't feel alone.
Because my roommate made me feel at home.

Coming of Age

When I was a child,
I called on the world to join me.
Later on in my life,
It was something to see.
I knew they would love me,
Along with God above thee.

When I was a child,
I called on the world to join me.
And people in my life would later see.
All of my friends and family, they led.
I did not know that one day I would be dead.

She Set Me Free

She set me free.
What is she going to do with anyone else but me?
We will wait and see. We will wait and see.

She will not say goodbye, with her frail voice plea.
We will later find out from her,
What she is going to do without me.
We will wait and see. We will wait and see.

Fresh Start

I want to be here
When it all comes in so clear.
I want to make a fresh start
So our love won't get old and part.
Maybe I will try a new religion
With God or Buddha or someone.
How about trying a new drug?
Unfortunately, that has already won.

Life

I want laugh.
I want to cry.
I want to live.
I want to die.

I want to say hello.
I want to say goodbye.
This must be my turn at life.
So I might have to think twice.

I See Red

I had a red vision one day.
That is all in my head, they say.
Yeah man, Frankie, you were right
It happened one night.
Here is where I think twice.

It could have been a spell I fell under.
It could have been a hot flash.
But the vision I saw was fast.
For just a few moments, it did not last.

It was me seeing red.
It was probably my dad playing with my head.
It could have been an LSD flashback.
You know if you try that stuff, you won't last.
Whatever it was, I know I will never see it again.
I just carry on the best I can.
It was almost as bad as getting struck by lightning.
The odds of that happening twice are frightening.
After this poem is said and done,
I wonder if it was an alien abduction of someone.

Listening to the Singer

Listen to the singer when he sings his songs.
He is trying to tell us something.
Maybe telling us what we are doing is wrong.
He sings about the blues.
He sings about his highs.
He may even sing a song about you.

Little Boy, Little Girl

Little boy, little girl
Walking down the street.
They held such a space, such poise, such face
And no defeat.
When we met, they led me on in prayer
And Jesus came into my heart to save me.
The devil was beat!
Little boy and little girl walking…
Walking down the street.

Offshore Drilling

Offshore drilling
You know how I'm feeling.
I don't agree about it.
And I don't feel free about it.

Too much of nature will be destroyed.
The dead birds, fish, and wildlife
We cannot ignore.
The sand will be covered,
The beaches with black oil.
I am sitting back like a snake
Ready and coiled.

The oil out on the Texas shoreline
They call it black gold or Texas tea.
All the wasted oil spills out there are too much for me.
Too hard to believe.

It Isn't True

If you have lived before in a past life,
Then you are not going to live again in a future life.
You can't live another life.
You don't live twice.

It is not going to happen again.
We are living in the present, man.
But when we have this feeling of "déjà vu"
We think it could be a sign,
A sign from our past life.
But remember then, we don't live twice.
Therefore, "déjà vu"
Isn't always true.

Look Out for the Mad Man

When he looks at you with fire in his eyes
Look out for the mad man when he cries.
Don't look back at him if you want to remain the same
Because he will cut you, and not take the blame.

Look out for the mad man when he cries!!
They have stabbed his heart with jealousy and grief.
He is slowly dying in someone else's world of make belief.
So when he looks at you with fire in his eyes
Look out for the mad man when he cries.

What are You?

Did you know there is a difference between some of us?
Some of us are fat, some of us are thin.
When are we ever gonna win?
Some of us are black, white, yellow, or red.
Didn't you know that most of that is all in your head?

They say the white boy is color blind.
Doesn't know the difference
Between black, red, white, or yellow.
That ain't a bad way to look at it, fellow.
If you ask me,
That is a good way to be.

The Jungle Master

You are the jungle master.
You know what they are after.
You have all the money of the jungle.
I mean, you have a bundle.

You are the jungle master.
Today the streets are faster.
Look out for a disaster.

You are the jungle master.
The drugs and weapons are coming faster.
What in the hell could they be after?
You are the jungle master.

Honey Hush

Honey hush, Honey hush.
You make such a fuss, girl.
I mean you are out of this world.
You stuck out in the crowd,
When you verbally attacked some poor child.
You know the people around can see you
Verbally attack some poor victim.
I mean you really do lick them.

Luckily these attacks don't get physical or out of control.
You are doing this act and it's growing old.
You had to be high when you sailed into that guy.
This time you took down a big one,
And he didn't think it was fun, son.

The Band

I am living in a hippy house
Where marijuana grows from its sprouts.
We have a rocking roll band that plays in the garage
And if you smoke enough weed, you will see the mirage.
Our band practices all day long
And we smoke more weed and all get along.

When we go out on the road to play
We will leave the house and load that day.
We will set our eyes and visions straight ahead
But still looking all around for Panama Red.
We will leave any troubles behind
And make sure we have a good time!

Young Lover

I was a young lover when I started out.
I could not say "I love you" to a girl.
I did not know how.
Or what is was all about.

Now that a few years have gone by.
And time has really flown by.
Now I can say "I love you".
As we grow old, and our love may never die.

The Pandemic

It's not all true, but it is true enough.
This thing is a damn pandemic,
And it ain't no gimmick!
This is the enemy.
It's the REAL thing that you cannot see, touch,
smell, or feel
But the symptoms can actually kill, also for real.

Hey man, stand six feet away from me!
I only have an allergy.
Air kisses, high fives
So we can all stay alive!

Will this thing ever come to an end?
I don't know, it's already been a while my friend.
I must avoid the crowd when I leave the house,
And they tell me to be aware of everything.
It's not over until the last sick lady sings.

Transcendental Meditation

Let me tell you about T.M.
It can be done in the a.m.
It can be done in the p.m.
Guess what? I learned it from a friend.

It helps with a good teacher,
Who sees no end
And we don't have to pretend.
There is really something to it.
Especially, when you begin.

You repeat a mantra over and over.
The words may have no meaning.
The mantra may have no closure.
Just slowly breathe in, and then breathe out.
Through your nose, and through your mouth.
It is easily done, without any doubt!!

The Girl Next Door

Little Lady, I FEEL you touch my heart when I call your name.
Little Lady, it's not that hard to explain.
Little Lady, we might be playing a game.
I chase you, you chase me.
That game isn't hard to see.

You left me for another person.
When I saw y'all together,
I was hurting.
We can still play the chase game, oh for certain.
And try so hard to forget about the hurting.

If it hurts you too bad,
Just remember the good times together we had.
That makes the hurting worthwhile.
You may even be able to manage a smile.

I know that you,
And the pain too,
Are not here to stay.
Little Lady, your name was an alarm in my heart.
Just hoping we would never part.

General Sherman

Did you hear the story about General Sherman?
He fought in the Civil War,
And he was NOT the good one!
Somewhere in Cheraw he held his headquarters.
The North would fight from there,
And he would give his orders.
Well, sooner than later,
A little boy from the South appeared on the scene.
He felt he knew Sherman.
He knew he was mean.

While the little boy sat on Sherman's lap,
He rubbed the top of Sherman's head
To see if he had horns and asked where they were at.
The little boy asked him if he was the devil.
The little boy, though, thought Sherman was incredible.

Hometown Legendary, Dizzy Gillespie

We had a family friend nicknamed Dizzy.
First name John and last name Gillespie.
He grew up in our home town of Cheraw.
And moved up north where people saw
Dizzy blow his trumpet like a king.
And I think his mother was actually a queen.

He was a famous composer, singer, and trumpet
playing man.
When he was up north and played in his band.
Someone fell on his trumpet one day,
And bent the bell upward.
I bet he felt like saying a cuss word.
It appeared to change his sound,
And made him an even better playing trumpet man.
He was the best around!

With his large balloon cheeks, he would play.
No one else could ever do it his way.
A bronze statue stands in his home town of Cheraw.
Seven feet high on Town Green, proud and tall.
His magical horn resides in a museum today.
With beautiful memories of how that famous man
could play!

www.ingramcontent.com/pod-product-compliance
Lightning Source LLC
LaVergne TN
LVHW091935070526
838200LV00068B/1270